AF420453

Book of Hope

Arvind Kumar

Copyright © Arvind Kumar 2024

All Rights Reserved.

ISBN 979-8-89363-954-4

This book has been published with all efforts taken to make the material error-free after the consent of the author. However, the author and the publisher do not assume and hereby disclaim any liability to any party for any loss, damage, or disruption caused by errors or omissions, whether such errors or omissions result from negligence, accident, or any other cause.

While every effort has been made to avoid any mistake or omission, this publication is being sold on the condition and understanding that neither the author nor the publishers or printers would be liable in any manner to any person by reason of any mistake or omission in this publication or for any action taken or omitted to be taken or advice rendered or accepted on the basis of this work. For any defect in printing or binding the publishers will be liable only to replace the defective copy by another copy of this work then available.

Dedication

To Nostalgia Mom
(My First Holy Teacher and the Reason for my Thought)

PREFACE

My son, Arvind Kumar, a young man with severe speech impairment, defied societal norms by schooling himself through unconventional means, and communicating his learnings via a computer keyboard from a young age. Despite lacking formal education, he showcased remarkable linguistic and computational skills, expressed through his diverse writings. He started expressing himself as early as the sixth year through typing, but he always typed only when I was around and when I touched his hands. Gradually he was typing with my hands just placed on his shoulders or back.

Arvind's thoughts and observations were compiled and brought out as a journal called "NEAT PORTRAIT" in December 2019.

He later started typing when I was not around, but he is now comfortable with only a trainer at Gurukulam (Mercy Angel).

I am amazed at his vocabulary, at times, wondering his source of learning as a person who had not pursued formal education. As he expressed his wish to interact with people a few months ago, we had collected questions from various persons across age groups, educational backgrounds, to which Arvind has responded and these responses are simple sometimes and philosophical, at most times, which are compiled in this book.

He himself chose the titles for both the English and Tamil version of the book.

Supriya has been the person who constantly motivated him in his work and I am grateful to her.

His story challenges stereotypes about the specially-abled, urging society to embrace empathy and provide equal opportunities for their integration into mainstream institutions.

Arvind's journey exemplifies the potential for individuals with disabilities to contribute meaningfully to society if given the chance.

The art work in the cover page of this book is also done by a person with autism, Daniel Christopher John.

I am extremely thankful to music therapist, Lakshmi ma'am, for encouraging him, appreciating his work, making efforts in understanding his perceptions of each of his responses and translating it into the Tamil language while maintaining the original perception of the text thoroughly.

Through "The Book of Hope" Arvind aims to represent his community, aiming to spread positivity and ultimately heal the world.

With Love

Radha Nandakumar (Arvind Kumar's mother)

INTERACTIONS

How did you feel when a neat portrait was released on stage?

Pretended to love on stage.

Would be your advice to anyone who is inspired by you?

Be passionate about good things.

Your thought on friendship?

A true friend never backstabs.

What impresses you the most?

Foremost love.

What makes you feel empowered?

Kind society.

What makes you most angry about our country?

More rapists.

Are you easy on yourself?

Even though expectations hit me hard, If it is without any societal judgement, I am always easy on myself.

What do you love to practice?

Strength of will in tenacity.

Judge a man by his?

Forbearance of patience.

Your views on addiction?

Better etiquette will engage in possible life.

What do you feel about agriculture?

Agriculture is India's dorsum.

Do schools kill creativity?

Absolute yes.

If you want anyone from Gurukulam to present a ted talk. what topic should they talk about?

Compulsive behaviours

How do you perceive "should i, should i not"?

Both are fictional.

Why do you pluck leaves from the garden?

Soon it will rejuvenate. I look deep in the green.

If you get a time machine, what will you do with it?

I will travel to my future and see the good in me and will cherish in present.

If you believe in rebirth, what would you want to be reborn as?

Rebirth as a normal homosapien.

What is karma according to you?

There is no karma in anyone's life.

Which is the best way to win violence?

Relax and accept the situation.

What is a dream job? what is yours?

A self-satisfied job. I would like to own an art gallery.

What do you want to learn in life?

I should learn to be a great listener.

Do you like to be alone or with people around?

With people who are not prejudiced.

Are you eager to write and communicate anything in particular to world? if so, what?

About my perception of life.

How do you perceive the five senses?

Sight of vision Taste of the Tongue Touching the skill
Feel the pain physically Strong olfaction

The sight you enjoy?

The night and the streetlights.

What do you feel about current Indian political scene? (his perspective)

Corruption everywhere.

What is the importance of water as a resource? (his perspective)

Basic necessity on the earth.
Viability of the world.

What do you look forward to everyday?

A new day; learning new things.

What would you be doing if you had been not doing any work?

Starting a startup.

What do you want to be in 10 minutes?

Fairytale king.

What is the one thing you are most terrible at?

Environment crises.

What conspiracy theory do you believe in?

Mystery of D.B. Cooper
(Hijacking a Boeing 727 and parachuting from the plane mid-
flight before disappearing)

What is one superpower which you never want to have?

Mind reading.

What is your definition of a good human being?

Lending a helping hand.

What animate object do you want to eliminate from the Universe?

Crowd.

How do you interpret Ramayana (mythology or history)?

History.

What does Lakshman Rekha mean in life?

Lead to repugnant action.

What is the virtue we need to learn from Rama?

Virtuous.

Lakshmana?

Skilled archer.

Sita?

Being sublime.

Ravana?

Arrogant.

Hanuman?

Unswerving devotee.

Life lesson from Ramayana?

Love and esteem.

Which character from Ramayana do you relate to and why?

Hanuman, the rescuer.

What is the symptom of an enlightened human according to you?

Trigged by life changing events.

Right way to do any action is?

Calm and composed.

What is absolute reality?

A fake scenario in reality (illusion)

What stops us?

Our dysphoria stops us.

What can we do together that none of us can do alone?

Will enjoy unforeseen moments in life.

How do you interact with God?

By luminescence of holy.

How can I help you?

In the way of interaction.

Is it good to have a bucket list? what is in yours?

It is a thing everyone should have, enabling us to survive alone. Spreading awareness to mankind.

Do you have any guilt?

Troubling Radha {his mother} for my daily life survival.

What would you title this chapter of your life?

Scuffle in the beautiful.

If your current life is a dream, would you want to dream more or wake up?

Wakeup.

What is the unhealthiest thing you did today?

Escaped from a class today.

Importance of "why" in life?

Where clearance arises.

**"Love is the only rational act" means
what?**

Expedite to love more.

Why are people embarrassed with silence?

Agitation riposte.

Should believe what we see or what we feel?

What we feel.

What does the phrases "is this all I want? is something missing?" mean to you?

Initiates meaning in life.

Where does a teacher influence a student's life?

Evaluates robustness and weakness.

What do you look at outside your window?

The rushing of bushes.

**"Love each other or perish" what does
this mean to you?**

If you never allow love in your life, you will be downcast always.

**'Reaction' or 'response' which is better?
and why?**

Response. reaction will always hurt people. responding is
superior.

Which of your relationships need more love and care?

Maternal bond should have more love and care.

What is the best part of human body?

The brain and belly.

And the worst?

Appendix.

Most important lesson we should teach a child?

Sense of liability.
Should always treat others in analogous manner.

Do you lie?

Oh yes, LOL.

Is it ok to lie? if so, why?

Yes, to save someone or to save yourself.

What is your best character trait?

Optimism in censorious situation.

What motivates you to wake up?

Thinking today everything will be fine.

Is failure important in life?

Of course, it is important.

How do you suggest we experience failure?

Should accept unfeigned.

What takes the most amount of time in your day?

Analysis.

What is the mythical creature that influenced you the most and why?

Lochness monster. (Underwater creature) It is a solitary survivor.

What is the one thing you never want to share no matter what?

That is a secret hehe..lol

Which is better to listen to, the heart or the brain?

The Heart. The Brain is always selfish.

What is your role in this life?

A healer.

A character from Mahabharata that is inspired you the most and why?

Sakuni, The game changer.

Do you want your biography written and what it should be named as?

Survive In Floundering.

What do you know way too much about?

Thinking as too much, yes, the way as too much.

Any academic subject you want to learn?

Geography

According to you, to live happily, does one need intelligence or emotions?

Both are fundamental things in life.

When sun is so hot why is space so cold?

They do not collide with each other.

Three things which India has to be proud of?

1. Civilization of heritage.
2. Industrialization.
3. Food grains.

What is the most important quality of a leader?

Reconcile.

What can be broken but never held?

Inferiority complex.

Man can do anything he wants? is that true?

Yes, it is, a Russian jailer survived 25 days without sleep.

When you are clever you change the world, when you are wise you change?

When the perception clever changes wisdom reigns

If you want to keep two possessions with you, what would it be?

Complexity of gallantry and high valour.

What feels like love to you?

Abiding inhale.

If you want to witness any event from past, present, or future. what would it be?

Events from the Middle Ages.

What or who really tires you and why?

More therapy, engaging in trauma.

What has five fingers but is not a hand?

Glove.

What does risk mean? what quality should you have to take risk in life?

Exposure to situations, to be outspoken. (ready to face)

What is our duty towards the nation?

To cherish our opulence and to respect our nation.

Who misutilises the freedom of speech the most?

Ambivalent people.

Why do you think God created man?

To show generosity.

Freedom gives us?

Gives natural liberties.

Om effect on thoughts?

Emanates peace.

How important is Bhava Spandana?

Insight of wisdom.

What did you learn from your father?

Amenability.

What does fire teach us?

Fire is the punisher of sin.

Quotes

Always be ecstatic in life.
Positions never decide endowment.

How can you embrace your weirdness?

With covered smile.

What skill would you like to master?

Psychic, telepath.

What are your beautiful memories of Delhi?

The slides of wind.

What mythological character do you relate to and why?

Hestia. Her Chastity.

What do you want to collect in your lifetime?

Abiding moments.

What is one thing you never do again?

Hurting others.

Quality in a friend you look for?

Unjudging foodie.

Any concerts you wish to attend?

Hate crowds.

What is your mantra?

Serenity and benevolence.

If you get a crystal ball to see your future what would you look for?

Will see I'm alive or not.

How do you handle demotivation?

Be far from those demotivating people.

What is the quality of a leader?

Sovereignty.

How should we handle imperfection?

There is no imperfection in human beings.

How important is gratitude, do you express it every day?

Gratitude is not important, it is healthy.
Of course, I do express.

What are you grateful for?

Aliveness.

Is it difficult for you to handle change?

Hard to accept.

What is the role of authentic connections in life?

Comfortable to reveal our vulnerable and true self.

What is a most important quality a woman has to develop according to you?

They are developed. They just have to accept their emotions.

How to take care of emotions?

Be careless of emotion.

How do you see divinity?

Nourishing wellbeing, sanctity.

What would you give away to achieve something?

Will give away my vexation.

What is boredom? and what do you do when you get bored?

When I have nothing to do.
I always engage myself by thinking about unrealistic things.

How does forgiving help us?

Helps in achieving tranquillity.

What does a profound experience mean to you?

Passive deliberation.

How do you deal with past guilt or regrets?

Mind always ponders, try not to recollect.

What's toughest thing for you?

Revive myself, wide away in conscious.

What will you get when you don't read other's mind?

Will get humdrum. (monotonous)

How do you deal with a person who hurts you?

I will never hurt them.

What gives you joy?

Panner is wholesome

What does the colour black represents?

Bravery.

Deep breathing helps in?

Releases anxiety.

What is your opinon on changing indias name to Bharath?

We are Bharathians.

What does feel learn and grow (Gurukulam's tagline) mean to you?

Its influential.

What does a lighthouse mean to you?

Faraway, astute.

Skill or studies which do you feel will have better scope in the future?

Skill is our world's future.

How to go from Dvaitha to Advaitha?

Stay in advaitha.
Nothing is enduring.

What are we learning from online education?

It's a smart move.

Most important quality of a doctor?

Tolerance and calmness.

Inquisitiveness helps us in?

Inexorable.

Love as an emotion can be explained as?

Love is well fortified.

How important are multiple choices in life?

Crucial, needed.

Write lines of appreciation to yourself?

The way I value others is appreciable.

Your experiences with strangers?

Strangers showing love towards me while they see me.

What conversation you enjoy the most?

Gossiping.

How important is it to fill our cups before giving energy to others?

Giving energy to others before you fill your cup.

What is something that you have done that makes you proud?

I am never proud of myself.

Write a love letter to your body for what all it does to you?

The vociferate was temporary. The torso of body was quirky. What else do I need I am abiding in love.

MY OBSERVATIONS

When action is swift.

Mistakes are certain.

When action is annoying..

Enemies are certain.

When action is dreadful.

Disaster is certain.

When action is appropriate.

Success is certain.

Quotes

Unless one make efforts, one cannot be successful.

Making efforts takes patience.

Patience is the fruit of practice.

Unless one has time, one cannot practice.

Nothing make people more happier than success.

Appreciation and applause follow.

What is the effect of Vishnu Sahasranam, how is it felt in the human brain?

Spiritual, saintly.

What are organs for?

To initiate the wellness

Orange colour reminds you of?

Wide wisdom

What does the eclipse remind us of?

Wants us to explore the bizarre.

Any mythological content or history you want to read about?

Aphrodite.

Why does lord Krishna play the flute?

For his happiness.

How do we break our comfort zone?

Learn new stuff.

Do the lines in our hands a have a meaning?

Prognosticate.

Quotes

Times of serenity enact.
People should be courteous to others.
Stance of disposition is always important.

What have you planned for your life?

Give my full efforts in my writing.

Your perception of attraction?

There is no purpose to attract.

How do we cleanse karma?

Do nothing.

How to accept surrender?

If you did wrong, surrender. Surrender is the best way for mental health.

Why do you love strong fragrances?

That's not too strong.

What is your idea of monkhood?

Eternity.

How to manifest?

By word twist.

Quotes

Catharsis is everything.

What does new year mean to you?

New start of bountiful year.

What is the unfulfilled dream?

Goa trip.

Biggest challenge you consider in a spiritual journey?

Negating bad thought.

What does Guru mean to you?

Spectacular, outspoken. {Arvind as guru} Next to God. {generally}

Who is your Guru?

Radha Nandakumar (His Mom).

What did you learn from your dad?

Being an unhesitating passionate worker.

Who are your biggest influences in your life?

People with healthy minds and thoughts.

What is your favourite childhood memory?

Hearing mom's narration about space.

What's joy to you?

1. Thinking deep.
2. love for literature.
3. Being happy for others.

What does perfection mean?

A human cannot be perfect.

What do you think about Har Ghar Tiranga, does it make sense to you?

Har Ghar Tiranga must be in every citizen's house. If it is in our hearts, that's also enough.

Quotes

Don't let your emotions spoil your dignity.

A day you don't like to remember in your life?

No reminisce, no regrets.

How do we balance work and life?

Be composed, both should never strike your mental health.

What gives you inner peace?

Simply, lucid things.

What is your idea of a fulfilling life?

Even merchants cannot fulfil their lives. Live your life lively.

Team leader should be?

Culpability.

How has interactive sessions with people changed you?

My thoughts are shared.

What is your dream?

My dream is to have diverse library.

What should we all be thankful for?

To experience the beautiful world.

Do you want a second chance about anything in life?

No. I'm happy now.

Quotes

Be hopeful all the time.

What's divinity?

Inner quality of affability and serenity.

What's water for a being?

Non skippable thing.

How to embrace uncertainty?

Desire of prompting, helps in sad glitch. (We look for prompts when we face uncertainty)

Can we reframe incidents in our life?

Pivoting in the present is the thing.

What's reflective listening?

Good mastery of perception.

Margazhi means what?

Month is full of glimmering merriment, lights in vibrant ritual, for me it's a food carnival hahaha lol.

What can we learn from our diverse minds?

Benevolence.

How to transform insight into action?

Wide motive thoughts.

Is there anything you would like to achieve now?

To be an uncanny man forever.

Holding resentment towards others leads to?

Return by dereliction.

How to handle an attention seeker?

Never give attention, this will help you receive favourable outcomes.

Everything in our lives stem from?

Deep evolution.

An aspect of life you need to seek?

Tolerance.

Why do bad things happen for good people?

Everyone is underneath God, so good being is here.
(Everything is God's will)

Do humans have freedom of choice or is everything predetermined?

Choice.

If we master mind , mind and energies we master?

Inner soul.

Quotes

Making amends, expiation is needed.

What does cross means in Christianity?

Torment of Holy Spirit for the people.

Why do you think vegetables have colours?

It has vitamins.

Why do you think leaves have different shapes?

Mutate in nature.

What does spiritual books teach you?

Be placid.

What does light and darkness mean ?

Unruffled.

What's love?

Cannot express.

What's peace?

Some inner satisfaction.

What is your opinion of giving God a form?

Showing love in sculpture.

Quotes

Armistice need vital in combat countries.

What would be your storyline for a short film?

A story of inexplicable inmost soul.

How to handle pain?

Look where you spend your pain. If you have calibre, you can handle pain.

What is one rule you abide by in your life?

Should have wide and weird thoughts.

Can the true reality be expressed?

Can be expressed when our dramatic view point comes to fail.

What's Vicharana?

That's Vicharana, it is probing.

What is the meaning of mantra "Narayana Akila Guru Bagvan namaste"?

Interlude in wave float.

Touch makes us?

Feel good.

How do you see God (form or formless)?

Formless.

What do I pray to him?

Don't stop my air.

Quotes

Deep insight is healthy.

What's true freedom?

When people stop being offended by others opinions.

Comfort zone leads to?

Deficit of experiencing the wild.

What happens when you consume others energies?

Energy is to share with others, not for self-satisfaction.

When we are determined to learn what do we do?

Consuming console. (open to learning)

What happens when we breathe ,trust and let go?

Indeed we peep within.

Every situation should be?

Not as you think.

What is attention? (Arvind's perspective)

To give right people the right time.

What does butterfly remind you of?

Living and abiding life in short time.

Quotes

Live in the present.

Why are male and female beings created for? apart from reproduction?

Expressing bond of intensity and passion.

How unique is India when it comes to languages?

It is a depth of treasure.

What is the relevance of a calendar?

I never care, every day is bright.

What does Jallikattu mean to you?

Manpower, even Rome has an ox festival (fact).

What does electric switch mean to you?

Regulates the tip of electric frequency.

What is about the vegetable that attracts gifted children the most to cut it and cook it?

Shape of every vegetable and feel of the roots in a carrot

What does an electric switch mean to you?

I'm not an electrician.

Quotes

Weird and wide thoughts are always ultimate.

How does silence help?

Helps us sort out situations which we think are frustrating for a long time.

How do you perceive the fear of missing out?

Cold inner pain in mortality.

Loneliness is a common feel in youth today how would you reason it?

Creating fake scenario.

What's creation?

Born in mistakes.

What is the significance of a human's birth?

Avail oneself of pristine opportunity.

What's yoga?

Therapeutic.

What's inclusion to you?

Divergent eyes.

How can the school system bring joy into a child's life?

Facing all stages.

About Sai Bajan in Gurukulam?

Loud chants to peaceful Saibaba.

Your feel about the harmonium (instrument)?

Among everyone I played well Brain never jams.

How did you feel deciding on the menu?

(Arvind decided his days menu) My inner joy fulfilled.

What does respect mean?

Basic gesture every human must have.

What should our hand remind us?

To feel the earth's body and roots.

Your ears remind you of?

To hear gossip, like an Elephant.

Why was the rat chosen as a Vahan of Ganapathi?

Ask Ganesh, lol.

What does Republic mean?

To announce Indian Legacy, demonstration of how we built our monetary system.

How can you experience God daily?

Breath of Wind.

How important is humility, how does it help?

Bold (courage/strength), yes verve (spirit) of entity.

What does a elephant remind you?

Augment of bravery.

Do you think it is necessary to imbibe God's quality in us?

Yes absolute.

What would be your recommendation to the state government for differently abled children?

Education should reach those living in poverty and make one an able person.

How do you perceive happiness?

Mental state is HAPPINESS.

What are the activities you recommend to Gurukulam which will help in differently abled child empowerment?

Should concentrate on vocational activities.

Why is mango called king of fruits according to you?

Its palatable.

When we watch a game what virtue can we learn?

1. Enthusiasm
2. Self Discipline
3. Teamwork
4. Cheering Others on.

When you look at earth it reminds you of?

Polite Serenity. Humans spoiling the planet.

ABOUT THE AUTHOR

Arvind Kumar, was born on 5th September 1996, in New Delhi. He was born with all normal parameters but started displaying symptoms of autism around the age of 3. Arvind has faced many challenges in his young life, besides his disabilities. He lost his older brother when he was 7 years old and lost his father when he was 14 years old, who was his main support and fan. This led to his relocation to Chennai. Arvind has always been an avid listener and his grasp of languages, especially English, has been exemplary. He was introduced to computers at the age of five and that opened up a new level of expression and learning for him. His ability to communicate effectively, has helped in generating new findings in the avenue of Autism. His understanding of human nature, sense of humour and his earnest wish to learn and break boundaries are evident in his writings.

He has completed class 12 in the open schooling system. He went ahead to complete a Diploma in Hotel Management and also tried learning photoshop and html coding. His ambition is to be an author, and be an individual counsellor in the future and heal the world.

ARTWORK

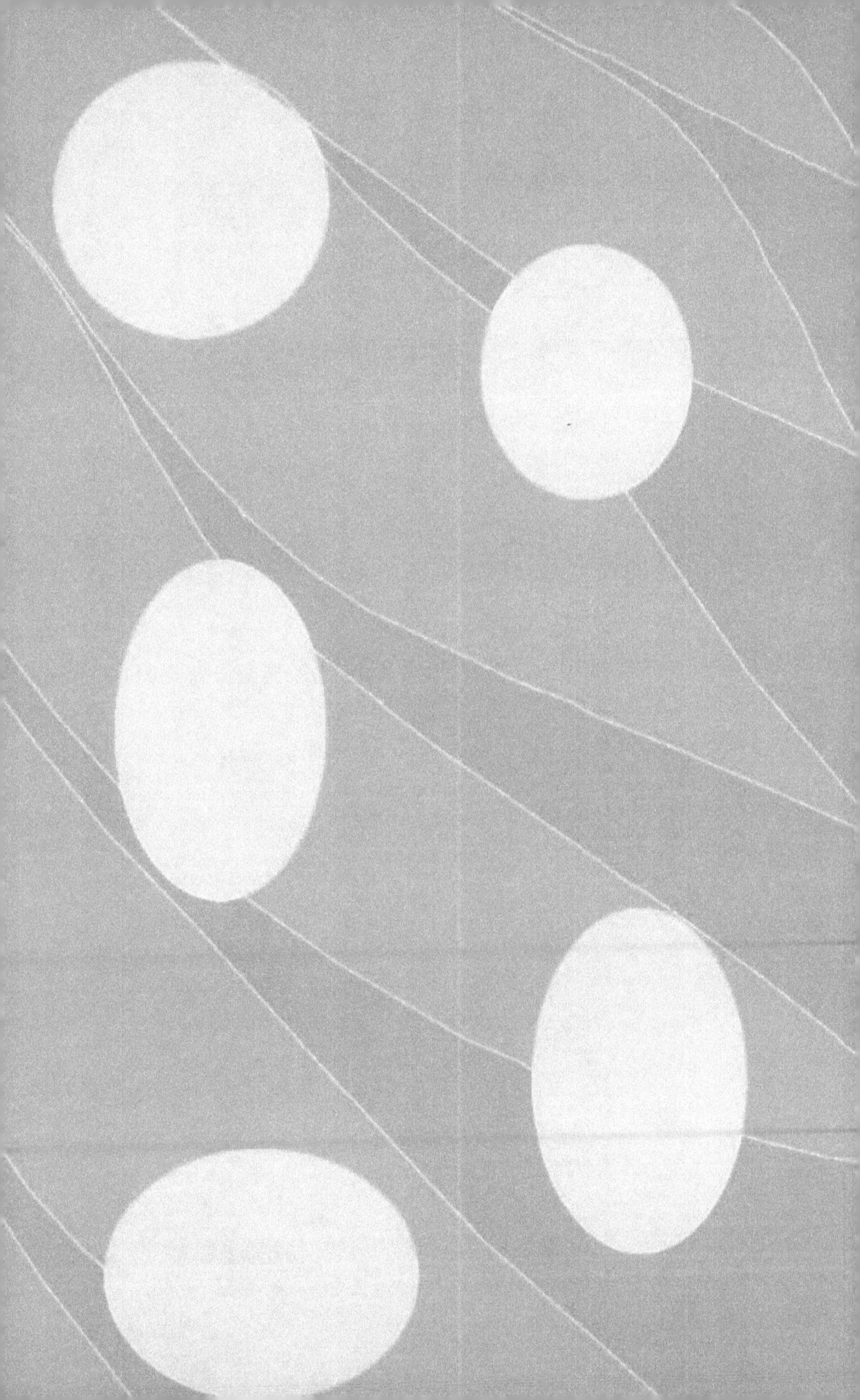